Folk Proverbs and Riddles

North American Folklore

Children's Folklore
Christmas and Santa Claus Folklore
Contemporary Folklore
Ethnic Folklore
Family Folklore
Firefighters' Folklore
Folk Arts and Crafts
Folk Customs
Folk Dance
Folk Fashion
Folk Festivals
Folk Games
Folk Medicine
Folk Music
Folk Proverbs and Riddles
Folk Religion
Folk Songs
Folk Speech
Folk Tales and Legends
Food Folklore
Regional Folklore

North American Folklore

Folk Proverbs and Riddles

by Autumn Libal

Mason Crest Publishers

Mason Crest Publishers Inc.
370 Reed Road
Broomall, Pennsylvania 19008
(866) MCP-BOOK (toll free)
www.masoncrest.com

First printing
1 2 3 4 5 6 7 8 9 10
Library of Congress Cataloging-in-Publication Data on file at the Library of Congress.
ISBN 1-59084-343-6
      1-59084-328-2

Design by Lori Holland.
Composition by Bytheway Publishing Services, Binghamton, New York.
Cover design by Joe Gilmore.
Printed and bound in the Hashemite Kingdom of Jordan.

Picture credits:
J. Rowe
Cover: "Will Rogers" by J. C. Leyendecker © 1940 SEPS: Licensed by Curtis Publishing,
      Indianapolis, IN. www.curtispublishing.com

Contents

Folklore grows from long-ago
seeds. Just as an acorn sends
down roots even as it shoots up
leaves across the sky, folklore is
rooted deeply in the past and
yet still lives and grows today.
It spreads through our modern
world with branches as wide
and sturdy as any oak's;
it grounds us in yesterday even
as it helps us make sense of
both the present and the future.

Introduction

by Dr. Alan Jabbour

W HAT DO A TALE, a joke, a fiddle tune, a quilt, a jig, a game of jacks, a saint's day procession, a snake fence, and a Halloween costume have in common? Not much, at first glance, but all these forms of human creativity are part of a zone of our cultural life and experience that we sometimes call "folklore."

The word "folklore" means the cultural traditions that are learned and passed along by ordinary people as part of the fabric of their lives and culture. Folklore may be passed along in verbal form, like the urban legend that we hear about from friends who assure us that it really happened to a friend of their cousin. Or it may be tunes or dance steps we pick up on the block, or ways of shaping things to use or admire out of materials readily available to us, like that quilt our aunt made. Often we acquire folklore without even fully realizing where or how we learned it.

Though we might imagine that the word "folklore" refers to cultural traditions from far away or long ago, we actually use and enjoy folklore as part of our own daily lives. It is often ordinary, yet we often remember and prize it because it seems somehow very special. Folklore is culture we share with others in our communities, and we build our identities through the sharing. Our first shared identity is family identity, and family folklore such as shared meals or prayers or songs helps us develop a sense of belonging. But as we grow older we learn to belong to other groups as well. Our identities may be ethnic, religious, occupational, or regional—or all of these, since no one has only one cultural identity. But in every case, the identity is anchored and strengthened by a variety of cultural traditions in which we participate and share with our neighbors. We feel the threads of connection with people we know, but the threads extend far beyond our own immediate communities. In a real sense, they connect us in one way or another to the world.

Folklore possesses features by which we distinguish ourselves from each other. A certain dance step may be African American, or a certain story urban, or a certain hymn Protestant, or a certain food preparation Cajun. Folklore can distinguish us, but at the same time it is one of the best ways we introduce ourselves to each other. We learn about new ethnic groups on the North American landscape by sampling their cuisine, and we enthusiastically adopt musical ideas from other communities. Stories, songs, and visual designs move from group to group, enriching all people in the process. Folklore thus is both a sign of identity, experienced as a special marker of our special groups, and at the same time a cultural coin that is well spent by sharing with others beyond our group boundaries.

Folklore is usually learned informally. Somebody, somewhere, taught us that jump rope rhyme we know, but we may have trouble remembering just where we got it, and it probably wasn't in a book that was assigned as homework. Our world has a domain of formal knowledge, but folklore is a domain of knowledge and culture that is learned by sharing and imitation rather than formal instruction. We can study it formally—that's what we are doing now!—but its natural arena is in the informal, person-to-person fabric of our lives.

Not all culture is folklore. Classical music, art sculpture, or great novels are forms of high art that may contain folklore but are not themselves folklore. Popular music or art may be built on folklore themes and traditions, but it addresses a much wider and more diverse audience than folk music or folk art. But even in the world of popular and mass culture, folklore keeps popping up around the margins. E-mail is not folklore—but an e-mail smile is. And college football is not folklore—but the wave we do at the stadium is.

This series of volumes explores the many faces of folklore throughout the North American continent. By illuminating the many aspects of folklore in our lives, we hope to help readers of the series to appreciate more fully the richness of the cultural fabric they either possess already or can easily encounter as they interact with their North American neighbors.

"Let sleeping dogs lie," is a tiny piece of wisdom called a proverb.

ONE

Bite-Size Pieces
of Folklore
What Proverbs and
Riddles Teach Us

What if every bit of cultural knowledge was blown straight out of your head?

*I*MAGINE THE following fantasy:

A young girl was cheerfully walking down a country lane. Suddenly the wind blew so hard that it knocked her down, and all the girl's thoughts tumbled out of her head. The thoughts were light like feathers and round like pebbles on the seashore. When she tried to catch her thoughts, they became liquid like water and ran away through her fingers.

As the girl stood up on thin shaking legs, she was very frightened, because she could not remember who she was or where she came from. A deep quaking filled her body and mind. She felt terrified, lost, and alone.

When she saw a young boy approaching, she ran up to him. Her voice shimmered with desperation as she asked, "What is my name, and who am I?" The boy looked puzzled, then laughed.

"Is this another riddle, Simone? The answer is too easy. Come on. I'll race you home!" And with that he was off, sprinting down the road. Simone could not believe the boy had ignored her question. Not knowing what else to do, she went running after him, hoping he would lead her home.

Up ahead, the boy turned and disappeared into a small brown house. Simone stopped on the stoop. The door to the house stood open, groaning in the wind. Simone peered through the dark doorway. "Wait!" she called. "Don't leave me. I don't know which house is mine."

"Dad! Simone's being stupid," she heard the boy call. "She

"You can lead a horse to water, but you can't make him drink," is a common proverb.

must have run out of real riddles because now she's asking really dumb ones."

"Don't call your sister stupid," a man's voice replied. "Simone, come inside now. It's getting dark."

Simone looked around at the quiet road. Not a person was in sight. Everything was gray and chilled with dusk. Simone hugged away a shiver and went inside.

She sat down on a chair and thought. Her name must be Simone, and she must live in this house. The boy, who was already starting to annoy her, must be her brother, and the kind-sounding man must be her father. But even though she knew this, she still felt lost.

The man walked into the room. He looked strong and knowing. Simone thought he would surely be able to tell her who she was.

"Dad," Simone said slowly, "who am I?"

Her father looked at her curiously. "Are you asking me a riddle? Well, this seems like a pretty easy one." He thought for a moment, then smiled. "Aha! I've got it! You are Simone."

"No, Dad," Simone said in frustration. "I'm not playing a game. I know my name is Simone, but who am I?"

"Let's ask your mother. Beth," her father called, "Simone has a riddle for you." Simone's mother entered the room. Simone thought this woman looked confident and smart. She would surely know who Simone was.

"Mom, I want to know who I am. Who am I?"

Her mother thought for a few minutes. "That's a difficult riddle, Simone. I don't know. What's the answer?" she asked, smiling.

"No, Mom! It's not a riddle! I want to know who I am." Now Simone was very upset. She was almost yelling, and hot tears filled her eyes. Her bewildered parents looked at each other questioningly.

"I think someone is overtired," her father said with a wink. "Come on, Simone. It's time to go to sleep. Go kiss Grandma goodnight, and get ready for bed." Simone looked down the hallway to where her father was pointing. Feeling defeated and alone, she walked down the hall to the tall, dark door. Her feet felt heavy, and teardrops splashed on her toes.

As she was about to knock on the old door, a creaky voice called out, "No need to knock. Come in, Simone." Simone stopped, slightly frightened, then twisted the knob and peered

"The early bird gets the worm," is a proverb based on a metaphor.

PROVERBS AS METAPHORS

Proverbs are often difficult to understand because of their metaphorical meanings. Here are some examples of metaphorical proverbs:

A bird in the hand is worth two in the bush.
A friend in need is a friend indeed.

What do they think these proverbs mean? Can a proverb have more than one meaning?

into the room. A wrinkly old woman sat on the bed, bathed in the yellow glow of her reading lamp. The woman patted the mattress beside her.

"Come sit here, and tell me what's bothering you."

Simone let go of the door and ran to the bed. She jumped up, threw her arms about her grandmother's waist, and buried her head into the pillowy softness of her grandmother's stomach. "Grandma, I can't remember who I am, or who Mom and Dad and my brother are. I can't even remember who you are. I keep asking people to tell me who I am, but they think I'm asking them a riddle. They just tell me that my name is Simone."

"Oh, I see dear," her grandmother said, smoothing her hair with a strong, steady hand. "You want to know who you really are, and that's a much bigger story than just your name. You are not just Simone. You

are sweet, gentle, charming Simone. You need to know your history to understand who you are. Brilliant, quick-witted, fun-loving, courageous Simone, let me tell you your history."

Simone and her grandmother talked deep into the night. The old woman told Simone stories about who her ancestors were, where they came from, what they had hoped for, the things they believed in, and the lessons they had learned during their lifetimes. As Simone listened, she began to understand where she came from and to remember who she was. The stories her grandmother told replaced all the thoughts that had flown away.

After many hours, her grandmother said, "Simone, I think that is enough for one night. You cannot know yourself in just one day. That takes many years."

Simone was amazed by all her grandmother had told her. "Grandma, you know so much. How do you remember all these things?"

"Simone, an old saying goes, 'A people without a history is like wind over buffalo grass.' If we do not remember our history, we will all scatter about the earth, faceless and voiceless

"You scratch my back and I'll scratch yours," is a contemporary American proverb.

Jan Harold Brunvand divides proverbs into different categories:

The *true proverb*, which is always a complete sentence expressing a general truth or wisdom, varies only slightly in form as it is passed along. Examples include those based on well-known fables or stories, such as "Don't count your chickens before they hatch," or "Don't kill the goose that lays the golden egg," and those which describe an act or event, such as "A rolling stone gathers no moss," and "A burnt child dreads the fire."

The *proverbial phrase*, which is never a complete sentence, varies a great deal, seldom expresses general wisdom and is almost always metaphorical. Examples include "behind the eight ball," "a song and a dance," "to be in hot water," "cut off one's nose to spite one's face," and "shoot oneself in the foot."

Proverbial comparisons express likenesses by using the words "like" or "as." These include "red as a beet," "go like blazes," "tighter than a drum," and "lower than a snake's belly."

with no bonds to make us brothers and sisters. I remember the things my mother and father told me, and the things their parents told them. Now you must remember the things that I tell you so they will never be forgotten. Let me shorten the wisdom of these stories into proverbs—sentences that will always stick in your memory."

Simone smiled as she listened to the proverbs her grandmother told her. Some of them made her think a moment before she could understand; some made her laugh out loud; and others even made her feel a little angry. But

she knew no wind would ever be strong enough to take away what her grandmother had taught her. As long as she remembered her grandmother's words, she would always know who she was.

Some common proverbs:

> If it ain't broke, don't fix it.
> Monkey see, monkey do.
> Don't put all your eggs in one basket.
> Easy come, easy go.
> Too many cooks spoil the soup.
> Never put off until tomorrow what you can do today.
> You can lead a horse to water, but you can't make him drink.
> Where there's smoke, there's fire.
> Bad weeds grow fast.
> You can't have your cake and eat it too.
> Red sky at night, sailor's delight.
> Lightning never strikes twice in the same place.
> Still waters run deep.
> Necessity is the mother of invention.
> The buck stops here.

Don't forget to also think about the metaphorical meanings of these proverbs. The metaphorical message is the real wisdom the proverb brings to us.

A PROVERB IN RHYME

Them as buys meat, buys bones;
Them as buys land, buys stones;
Them as buy eggs, buys shells;
Them as buys ale, buys nothing else.

YOU probably take for granted the centuries of tradition and wisdom that shape your identity. But suppose you were to suddenly lose it all. Imagine how you would feel if you were Simone.

As Simone's grandmother said, "A people without a history is like wind over buffalo grass." This Native American proverb of the Sioux people emphasizes the importance of remembering one's culture and passing on the lessons that people have already learned to future generations. Many people believe that knowing the wisdom and history of a person's ancestors is important for understanding that individual's past, present, and future.

According to the proverb, "Time heals all wounds."

Today, we collect and preserve wisdom and knowledge in books, written documents, computers, and other forms of information storage. But long ago, languages were not written down; they were only spoken. In those times, people preserved their knowledge through **oral literature** and traditions. Unlike the literature you find printed in books, oral literature is not recorded in writing. Instead, oral literature is passed from person to person, using stories, poems, songs, jokes, proverbs, and riddles that are told by one person to another and by older members of the community to younger ones.

You might be surprised to know that in our modern times there are still groups of people who only have spoken languages with no form of writing or reading. In these groups, oral tradition is especially important. Even in many societies that do have written language, however, oral literature may be very important be-

CONTEMPORARY AMERICAN PROVERBS

Fish or cut bait.
Let sleeping dogmas lie.
Never trouble trouble till trouble troubles you.

cause education is not always widely available. In some countries, only the wealthiest people have enough money for things like school, books, and paper. Other people must depend on the oral traditions of the past for their education.

Even in places like America and Canada where basic education is available to almost everyone, oral traditions are evident all around us. Although libraries, universities, and the Internet are widely available, people still enjoy participating in the oral traditions of their past. Proverbs and riddles are especially important parts of oral tradition. For instance, begin to really pay attention, and you may

WISDOM AND FOLLY

Better a blow from a wise man than a kiss from a
    fool.
One fool can ask more questions than ten wise
    men can answer.
Do not ask the wise man, ask the experienced
    one.
Live and let live.
Don't throw salt on people's wounds.
A stranger's cloak does not keep one warm.

"People who live in glass houses shouldn't throw stones."

find that proverbs are all around you in your daily life. The next time you hear a proverb or someone asks you a riddle, remember it, and then tell it to someone else; you will be participating in the oral tradition.

WHAT IS A PROVERB?

It is not easy to define proverbs because they exist in various forms in different languages and cultures. Generally speaking, however, a proverb is a short, easily remembered phrase that contains general beliefs, knowledge, or wisdom. Proverbs contain a lot of meaning in just a few words. They are passed down from person to person through the generations, and often their meaning is **metaphorical**. An example of a metaphorical proverb is:

"People who live in glass houses should not throw stones."

This proverb is metaphorical because, although it uses the words "glass houses" and "stones," it is not actually talking about

According to the proverb, you can catch more flies with honey.

glass houses or stones. If it were talking about those things, the meaning would be **literal**. Instead, the proverb's actual meaning must be interpreted through some careful thought. Stones could break a glass house. If you live in a glass house yourself, you should not be breaking other people's houses because yours is just as fragile. But, of course, people do not live in glass houses. So what does this proverb really mean? Instead of being about glass houses, the lesson in the proverb is that a person should not be pointing out the faults of others if she has faults of her own.

WHAT IS A RIDDLE?

Whereas proverbs are sayings that contain pieces of knowledge, riddles often test people's wisdom and knowledge. Just as proverbs can come in various forms, there are many different kinds of riddles. Some riddles are just a question. Others may be in the form of a poem that ends with a question. Still other riddles may not ask a question at all. Instead, there can be a mystery tied up in the words of the riddle.

Riddles take many forms. Here are some examples.

Conundrums
Riddles that play with the sounds of words are often called conundrums. An example of a conundrum is:

"What is black and white and red all over?"

This conundrum plays with the word "red," which is a color. The word "red," however, sounds like the word "read," which is past tense for reading. What the riddle actually asks is, "What is black and white and *read* all over?" But, because the riddle is spoken (in the oral tradition) rather than written down, the recipient of the riddle generally makes the assumption that, because black and white are colors, the red/read being referred to must also be a color. Therein lies the confusion and the puzzle of the riddle.

(*Answer:* A newspaper—of course!)

Joke Riddles
Many riddles are meant to be intellectually challenging, but others are meant to just be funny. Often the joke in a riddle comes from its simplicity. A very common joke riddle is:

"Why did the chicken cross the road?"

This riddle becomes funny because its answer is so simple that the riddle is silly and laughable.

(*Answer:* To get to the other side!)

Throughout our folkloric history, riddles have been used for much more than just fun and games. Riddles, as challenges between minds, were sometimes used as seriously as duels with swords. There are many examples in literature of riddles as part of serious and dangerous mental duels. For example, in the fairy-tale of "Rumplestiltskin," the Queen must discover the riddle of the little man's name or he will take her child away. In J.R.R.

Tolkien's *The Hobbit*, Bilbo Baggins and Gollum battle with riddles. If Bilbo wins, Gollum will release him, but if Gollum wins, Gollum gets to eat Bilbo. It's a good thing Bilbo is a smart hobbit and a good riddler!

You will probably never need to win either the life of your child or your own life through solving a riddle—but like proverbs, riddles help us shape our world. They tease our brains and make us think. They may make us laugh. But most of all, they tell us something about who we are and how we see the world.

Many proverbs come from the Bible.

TWO

From the Bible to Benjamin Franklin

Proverbs Rooted in Written History

"Let he who has not sinned throw the first stone."

THE WOMAN STOOD alone and frightened in the dusty square. The crowds gathered in around her. They looked at her with disgust. They pointed their fingers and screamed insults. Some held hard stones in their hands.

Jesus and his followers walked into the square. Jesus turned to the seething mob and asked why they were gathered in anger. A man pointed at the woman and spoke, "She has committed a great sin. The law says we must kill her with stones, and that is what we will do."

Jesus looked at the frightened woman and asked, "My child, is what they accuse you of true?"

She lowered her eyes and nodded her head, "Yes, my Lord, I am guilty of great sin."

The crowd roared with anger and began scooping more stones from the earth. Jesus watched them as they shouted, waving their fists in the air. But he did not join in the crowd's anger. He did not scream or shout. He did not hunger for the woman's death. Instead, he quietly picked up a stick and began writing in the sand.

Slowly, the crowd grew silent. They turned away from the woman to see what Jesus was writing. (The story never tells what Jesus wrote in the dirt.) A man looked up at Jesus and asked what he was doing.

"According to the law, this woman shall be stoned for her sin," Jesus replied. "Let anyone who has not sinned cast the first stone."

The people looked first at Jesus, and then at the words he had written in the sand. Their hands loosened their grips about the stones, and the stones fell, harmless to the earth. The crowd dispersed and left the woman standing in the square. Instead of accusing and calling for the blood of others, each person considered his own faults and the sins he had committed.

THE BIBLE

The Bible is one of the oldest and most well-known sources of proverbs. The story above is told in the New Testament and illustrates the origin of the now common proverb, "Let he who has not sinned cast the first stone." Jesus presented many proverbial lessons, which are recorded in the New Testament. Some examples of his other proverbial teachings are, "Love your neighbor as yourself," "Do unto others as you would have them do unto you," and "Turn the other cheek." These sayings have become folk proverbs in their own right.

The Old Testament of the Bible is divided into sections which are filled with proverbial lessons. In fact, one entire section of the Old Testament is dedicated to proverbs and their explanations. Titled the Book of Proverbs, it contains proverbs like, "You reap what you sow," "A gentle answer turns away wrath, but a harsh word stirs up anger," and "A happy heart makes the face cheerful, but heartache crushes the spirit."

OTHER SPIRITUAL SOURCES

The Bible, of course, is not the only source of proverbs. Spiritual teachings of all types are rich with proverbial wisdom. For example, Martin Luther King, Jr., a great minister and leader in America's Civil Rights movement, said, "We must learn to live together as brothers, or perish together as fools." Gandhi, a great spiritual and political leader in India, restated the original Biblical saying "An eye for an eye" as "An eye for an eye makes the whole world go blind."

SECULAR LITERATURE

Books and teachings that do not have a religious connection are referred to as secular. One famous secular book containing proverbs is Benjamin Franklin's *Poor Richard's Almanac*. Benjamin Franklin, one of the signers of the Declaration of Independence and the inventor of such things as bifocal eyeglasses and the lightning rod, began publishing *Poor Richard's Almanac* in 1733. The **almanac** was famous, not only for its useful information, but for the many wise proverbs and sayings that Franklin

Benjamin Franklin is often given credit for this well-known proverb: "A stitch in time, saves nine."

sprinkled throughout its pages. Some examples of proverbs published in *Poor Richard's Almanac* are:

> "More men have been made slaves by their wealth than have been freed by it."

> "The things that hurt, instruct."

People often give Benjamin Franklin credit for creating all of the proverbs he printed. Though Benjamin Franklin did write many of the wise sayings that appear in his almanac, he certainly did not come up with all the sayings on his own. Many were already in common use in the oral tradition for generations before Benjamin Franklin published them. What Franklin did was record and popularize these pieces of wisdom by writing them in the almanac and making them available to large numbers of people.

BENJAMIN FRANKLIN

Benjamin Franklin was born in 1709 in Massachusetts. Although he only had two years of formal education, this intelligent, inspiring historic figure went on to become an inventor, a printer, and to speak six languages.

RELIGIOUS PROVERBS

The many religions in the world—religious traditions like Buddhism, Judaism, Islam, Christianity, Hinduism, Confucianism, and others— all offer proverbs. Do you think these bites of wisdom teach lessons that are different from each other—or are they similar? You might want to ask a friend of a different religion what religious proverbs he or she knows. Are they similar to the ones you know?

Here are some religious books where you can look for proverbs:

- the Torah (Judaism—the first five books of what Christians call the Old Testament)
- the Koran (Islam)
- the Bhagavad-Gita (Hinduism)

An old African proverb states, "In a court of birds, the bug never wins."

THE BIRTH OF A PROVERB

Even our oldest proverbs were once uttered for the first time. Sometimes in today's world someone says something so meaningful to masses of people that they begin to repeat it. Other times a well-known person repeats an original proverbial phrase so often that it becomes associated with him or her, and it too begins to be repeated by other people. Consider the following proverbial sentences. Do you think that people will still recognize and even be repeating them to each other years from now? Are they becoming proverbs?

Ask not what your country can do for you; ask what you can do for your country.
—*President John F. Kennedy*

Float like a butterfly; sting like a bee.
—*Muhammad Ali*

If a cluttered desk is a sign of a cluttered mind, of what is an empty desk a sign?
—*Albert Einstein*

If you can't take the heat, get out of the kitchen.
—*President Harry S. Truman*

All you need is love.
—*The Beatles* ("All You Need Is Love")

The wisdom of many, the wit of one.
—*one definition of a folk proverb*

Proverbs are the palm oil with which words are eaten.
—*Chinua Achebe*

Benjamin Franklin

• the Analects (the teachings of Confucius)
• the Spiritual Writings of Rumi (Sufism)

All these have used ancient folk proverbs—and they have created and kept folk proverbs alive in their words.

Other faiths, like many of the religions of Native American and African tribes, do not have written collections of their teachings, because until Europeans began to colonize their land, their languages were not written; their spiritual beliefs were kept in oral tradition. As millions of Native American and Africans died, their religions and unwritten beliefs died with them. Now, however, some of the surviving oral traditions have been recorded in the hopes that no more of these important histories will be lost. The library and Internet will offer you examples of proverbs from Native American and African traditions.

WHAT'S OLD IS NEW AGAIN

In our fast-paced world of technology and entertainment, some proverbs might, upon first hearing them, seem old or out of date. Ask your parents and grandparents if they remember any old proverbs. Look for more on the Internet or in books. What did these proverbs mean long ago? Do the proverbs have relevance in today's world? Are their new meanings different or are they the same as the old ones? For instance, consider an old proverb from the sayings of Jesus:

"Human beings do not live by bread alone."

What do you think the proverb means? Is it still true?

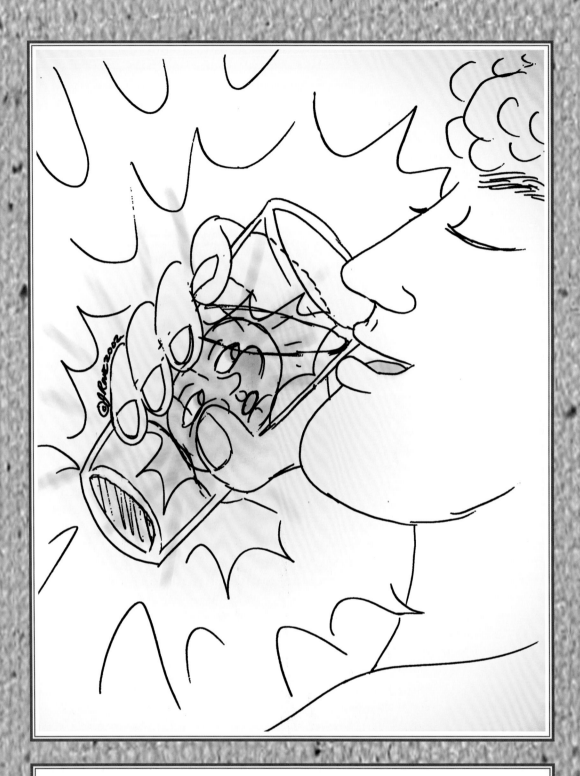

Sometimes folk proverbs and advertising slogans can blend. Do you recognize the ad behind this illustration? (Answer: "A day without orange juice is like a day without sunshine"— Florida Citrus Commission)

THREE

Using Words to Sell
Proverbs in Advertising

"When life gives you lemons, make lemonade," is good advice for consumers. The phrase "lemon" has come to mean a product that is unsatisfactory or defective.

I ONLY TURNED my television on for five minutes. I'm not addicted to the television set, and I wasn't going to watch very long. Most of what was on was commercials anyway. After all, how much harm can they be?

Then I decided to surf the 'Net for a while. It didn't matter that I had studying to do. After all, the Internet is an educational tool and highly informative to someone of my age, right? How can something so good be bad?

Then I had an itch to go out, just for a little drive. Billboards flashed on every mile of the road. My parents say the billboards ruin the landscape, but I don't think they are so bad, do you?

Suddenly, I found myself at the mall. I don't even remember how I got there. There was nothing I needed or wanted. But once inside, I wanted everything. There were great big stereos and little tiny cell-phones. There were posters of pop stars and shiny accessories. The kitchen store had tons of nifty gadgets (wait a minute . . . I don't even have a kitchen). Remembering that, I wandered over to the sports store that was having a "big spring blow-out sale" on skis. (I don't know how to ski, but I'd love to learn!) From mini-skirts to button-down shirts, from neckties to magazines, and from ten-person tents to lawn ornaments, they had everything a person could ever need—or want! And I wanted it! I wanted it all! I had become an advertiser's dream come true.

An advertiser's job is to promote a product. But with so many millions of things available on the market today, how can a company get our attention and convince us to buy its product instead

Early advertising also used slogans that were based on folk traditions.

of someone else's? The advertisers must convince us, the consumers, that their product is desirable, dependable, superior to other products, a real bargain for the price, and something we just can't live without.

One of the ways advertisers have found for getting our attention is to use proverbs in their advertisements. Proverbial sayings have a long history of meaning and wisdom with which people are familiar, that they already trust. By using a saying that people recognize and that they have accepted as truth, often for as many years as they can remember, companies can make a product feel as dependable and genuine as the proverb is. When such sayings are applied to a product, the seller's goal is to make the potential customer associate the product with all the timeless, trustworthy, and reliable messages embodied in the proverb.

PROVERB IMPERSONATION

Companies, however, do not limit themselves to using traditional proverbs in order to get us to trust and buy their products. Proverbs usually have a very specific length, pattern, and sound to them. Ad-

vertisers often promote their products by making up sayings that sound like proverbs, but actually are not proverbs at all. Since we are so accustomed to the sound of proverbs, we may not even notice that the **slogan** is not actually a real proverb. In our modern, advertising-filled society, these catchy phrases and slogans often become as well known to us as traditional proverbs are.

One of the differences you may notice between a saying that is actually a proverb and an advertising slogan that simply mimics a proverb is that the slogan only has a literal meaning. Proverbs usually have a metaphorical meaning beyond the literal words, but advertising slogans do not usually have wise metaphors that can extend beyond the product.

How advertising savvy are you?

Can you fill in the blanks?

"The milk chocolate melts in your _____ and not in your _____." (M&M's)
"A day without orange juice is like a day without _____." (Florida Citrus Commission)
"The best part of waking up is _____ in your cup."
"Like a good neighbor, _____ is there."

(*Answers:* mouth, hand
sunshine
Folgers
State Farm)

A COMMERCIAL IN DISGUISE

Here is just a short list of some of the many commercial slogans that have become "proverbs" of our modern culture. How many do you recognize?

"Be all that you can be." (the United States Army)

"A diamond is forever." (De Beers Consolidated Mines)

"Just do it." (Nike)

"Once you pop, you can't stop!" (Pringles Potato Chips)

"It takes a licking and keeps on ticking." (Timex Watches)

PROVERBS NOT INTENDED TO BE ADS

"Wake up and smell the coffee."

"Art imitates life."

"A penny saved is a penny earned."

"You can't judge a book by its cover."

"He who laughs last laughs best."

What is the intended meaning of each of these proverbs? How could these proverbs be used in an advertisement? How do the proverbs' meanings change when they are used this way?

CONTEMPORARY PROVERBS

New proverbs that have sprung up around the world of advertising are not always about specific products or companies. Some new proverbs show the same characteristics of traditional proverbs in that they display the "general wisdom" of a culture (in this case, the consumer culture of modern times). Examples are:

"The customer is always right."

"Let the buyer beware."

"You break it, you buy it."

"You can't take it with you."

"Here today, gone tomorrow."

"The best presents come in small packages."

Are these proverbs literal or metaphorical? Can you think of other modern proverbs?

Centuries of folk wisdom can supplement the modern medical world's understanding of health.

FOUR

Health is Better than Wealth
Medical Proverbs

An old folk proverb can sometimes point the way toward a better way of living.

JACK SPED ALONG the highway in his new red convertible. The cool wind fluttered his hair and the soft sun warmed his shoulders, but he didn't notice. The only thing Jack noticed was how the traffic was grinding to a halt and that the clock said 8:01 A.M. His car slowed to a standstill. Work started one minute ago, and Jack was still on the highway. "Great," he thought. "By the time I get there, I'll be 15 minutes late."

Sitting in the stopped traffic, Jack became anxious. He shifted in his seat, tapped his feet, and began drumming his fingers on the steering wheel. His shoulders tensed, and a headache pulsed behind his eyes. He turned on the radio to get a traffic report. A snappy tune was playing, but Jack wasn't listening to the music.

The music died away and the DJ came on, "Now, for all of you stopped out there in traffic, here's something to brighten your day. Do you have your cell-phone handy? I know you do. Call in the next five minutes with your favorite proverb or wise saying and you could win dinner for two at the restaurant of your choice. Better call in now. The phones are already ringing."

Jack looked at the radio and groaned. The DJ spoke back, "Our first caller has a great proverb for us this morning. She says we should all 'Stop and smell the roses' on this fine sunny morning."

Jack scoffed, "Yeah, maybe you can stop and smell the roses, but I've got to get to work. You can't have roses to smell if you have no money to buy them with."

"And here's another one for all you out there rushing to get to work," the DJ announced. "All work and no play makes Jack a dull boy." Jack looked at the radio and shook his head.

"Man, these people don't know what they're talking about. What do they expect to do for fun if they have no money to do it with?" Jack considered changing the station, but then the announcer caught his attention again.

"Our third caller and winner of a beautiful dinner for two has this proverb for us all. Her wise words are, 'Health is better than wealth.' Now for. . ." Jack groaned as he switched off the radio and the traffic began moving again.

By the time Jack got to work, his head was pounding and he felt sick to his stomach. He stared at his computer screen all day, the light of the monitor searing his eyes, but he forced himself to keep working. All he could think about was getting home and going to sleep. But five o'clock came, then six o'clock, then seven. Jack looked at the pile of work on his desk, took another aspirin, and pushed on. By the time he left his office, it was already dark outside, as usual.

When Jack walked through the door, his four-year-old son charged at him. "You're home! You're home! You're home!" his son cried. "I thought you were never going to get home. Can we play now?"

"Not right now, Timmy," Jack replied. "Daddy's really tired. I have to lie down."

"The head and feet keep warm and the rest will take no harm," is a proverb that recommends prevention as a good health strategy.

"Ohhh, but Dad," Timmy whined. "You promised."

"I'm sorry, Timmy. I just can't. I had a hard day. We'll play to-morrow."

"It's not fair!" Timmy's voice got louder. "You say that every day!" Timmy was starting to yell. "You said you'd teach me to ride my bike! All the other kids know how to do it already, and I don't. You're never going to teach me!"

"Timmy be quiet!" Jack was surprised to hear himself yelling back at his young son. "I'm sorry, Timmy, but I have a terrible headache. Be a good boy now. Why don't you go and play with your video games for awhile."

Timmy pouted and stamped away, angry and disappointed.

Jack went to his bedroom and collapsed. He felt terrible. His head felt like it could burst, his stomach churned, but something else was wrong as well. His closet door stood open. He glanced at the closet and noticed the rows and rows of expensive suits arranged according to color: black, gray, brown, blue, pants, shirts, suit jackets, and silk ties. He looked around his room at his king-size bed, his cell phone and pager on the night stand, the keys to his convertible on the dresser, the expensive watch on his wrist. He realized that he spent hours in bed with headaches, looking around this room. But suddenly he knew that this room held nothing worth looking at. He didn't love his suits or phone or car as much as he loved his son. He wished that it was earlier in the evening. He wished he didn't have such an awful headache. Where he really wanted to be was outside, teaching his son to ride a bike. But he couldn't go because it was too late

> **Proverbs with a medical meaning:**
>
> "An apple a day keeps the doctor away."
> "Laughter is the best medicine."
> "Time heals all wounds."
> "The first step to health is to know that we are
>   sick."
> "Nature, time, and patience are three great physi-
>   cians."
>
> Are these proverbs just about physical health, or do
> some of them have a broader meaning?

and he felt too sick. Then he thought back to what the woman on the radio had said that morning and thought, "Yes, health is better than wealth. I'm turning over a new leaf tomorrow morning."

PROVERBS, as pieces of general wisdom, commonly focus on issues of health and medicine. An example of a medical proverb is "Feed a cold, starve a fever." This proverb gives specific directions for treating colds and fevers, but most medical proverbs are not this specific. Most medical proverbs are quite general in their advice. They usually do not tell us how to cure individual illnesses. In-

stead, they remind us to value our health and give advice for preventing illness, for if there is no illness, there is no need of a cure. "Health is better than wealth" is an example of a medical proverb about the value of good health. "An ounce of prevention is worth a pound of cure" is a proverb that focuses on preventing illnesses rather than treating illnesses. We may have heard these proverbs so many times that at first glance they seem trite—but as Jack found, these proverbs contain genuine nuggets of wisdom, practical strategies for health and well-being.

The folklore of today can be the science of tomorrow.

Today, medicine has greatly advanced through science and research. One lesson we have learned is that fatty foods can be bad for us. High-fat foods contribute to things like high cholesterol and heart disease. The proverb "Butter is gold in the morning, silver at noon, and lead at night" shows that people already understood the dangers of some fatty foods even before they had the scientific research that proved this. Can you think of other proverbs that have been proven by modern science?

A HEALTHY MIND IN A HEALTHY BODY

Another interesting aspect of medical proverbs is that their advice often applies to more than the health of the physical body. What is good advice for a person's body, is usually also good advice for a person's entire life. For example, the proverb "A spoon full of sugar makes the medicine go down" suggests that medicine that tastes bad will be easier to swallow if sweetened with sugar. This can be true in the literal sense, but the proverb can also mean other things. If you had bad news to give to someone, you could do things to make the news easier to hear, like give the person a hug, offer to help her with the problem, or give comforting and supportive words. In this case, the bad news is like the medicine, and your help and comfort is like the sugar that makes the medicine easier to take.

PROVERBS AND PREVENTION

The traditions that shaped North America's folk proverbs were sometimes very different from today's practices. For instance, a hundred years ago or more, medical treatments were expensive and often ineffective; doctors were rare; and many illnesses were life-threatening. Many people depended more on prevention than treatment for their health. Here are some folk proverbs that express this philosophy:

"Early to bed, early to rise, makes a man healthy, wealthy, and wise."

"After dinner sit awhile, after supper walk a mile."

"Eat to live, not live to eat."

"Moderation in all things."

Medical practices today are very different from those of earlier times. In the United States and Canada we now have huge hospitals, research facilities working on cures for diseases, and drugstores lined with shelves of treatments for everyday aches and pains. Do you think modern medicine focuses more on prevention or cures? Do old medical proverbs still give valuable advice—or has modern medicine made them outdated? What do you think?

Sometimes you have to think for yourself. As the old proverbial question asks: "If everyone jumped off a bridge, would you jump off too?"

FIVE

"Good Fences Make Good Neighbors"
Proverbs That Have Traveled Far from Their Origins

Friends may need to respect their differences by setting healthy boundaries—while not letting high walls separate them from each other.

GOOD FENCES make good neighbors" is a popular proverb. But just because it has been repeated for centuries, does not mean that today's culture will understand the wisdom that originally shaped this saying.

For instance, some people might associate the story that follows with this proverb.

THERE once were two old men who had always lived as friends and neighbors. Each had his own plot of land and his own house, but they spent all of their time together. A stand of trees for firewood grew on the first man's land. The second man had two apple trees for making sweet apple cider. Where their land met, they had one large garden that they tended together in the mornings. Every evening, when their work was done, they sat to play a game of checkers before returning to their separate houses.

One day as they tended the garden, the first man said, "I have been thinking. Perhaps we should mark the line that divides our land."

The second man looked up from the rich soil he was turning. "Why should we mark the line that divides our land? We know where it is, and we have never needed to mark it before."

"That is true," said the first man, "but we are growing very old. What if our minds slip away just as our youth did? What if we wake up one morning and can no longer remember which land is mine and which land is yours?"

"Hmm, you are right," the second man said. "Let us build a

fence so we will always know the difference between your land and mine."

That day, instead of sipping cider and playing checkers, they built a fence that divided their land and separated their houses. On one side of the fence stood the stand of firewood. On the other side were the two apple trees. The fence ran through the middle of the garden making two gardens where before there had only been one.

The old men were very proud of their fence and began to en-

POSITIVE VS. NEGATIVE

Negative Proverb: "The burnt child dreads the fire."
(This proverb suggests that painful punishment is a good way to teach children correct behavior.)

Positive Proverb: "Tell me and I'll forget. Show me, and I may not remember. Involve me, and I'll understand."
(This Native American proverb emphasizes teaching over punishment. It also points out that it is not enough to simply remember a lesson. The most important thing is to truly understand what you are taught.)

"If wishes were horses, beggars would ride."

joy working on it more than they liked working in their gardens. Weeks went by, and each time the fence seemed finished, they found a new way to improve it. They built a fancy gate so that the first man could go pick apples from the second man's trees, and so the second man could go get firewood whenever he was cold. After the gate was complete, they decided to make the fence even higher. The fence grew so high that they could only see each other's eyes over the top.

The men liked the fence so much that they could not see how it was blocking the sun to the garden. The garden, now divided into two, was growing weak. No one watered or weeded it anymore because they were so busy working on their fence. As the men worked on the fence, they did not notice that all the plants in their garden were first shriveling and then dying and disappearing into nothingness.

Finally, the fence was complete. The next morning, the men went to their gardens and found that all the vegetables were gone. The men were very angry. Each man suspected his neighbor had stolen the vegetables during the night. They ran up to the fence and yelled at each other. "How dare you steal all the vegetables from my garden!" the first man bellowed.

"You are crazy!" the second man cried. "I did not steal the vegetables from your garden. You took them from mine!" They eyed each other suspiciously. Then they became very quiet.

"This garden used to be one large garden that belonged to both of us and that we cared for together," the first man said.

"Perhaps the vegetables died when we were working on the fence," the second man replied.

They were quiet for a long time. Each man knew the other had not stolen from him, but they could not forget their anger and suspicion.

"Perhaps we should put a lock on this gate just in case," one suggested and the other agreed.

The men were silent as they fastened the lock to the gate. When it was done, the first man sighed. "Maybe we can play checkers tomorrow, and everything can be as it was before."

That night it rained and rained. The next day the men met at the gate for their game of checkers, but when they tried to open the gate, they found that the lock had rusted shut. They looked at each other over the fence. "It has been so long since we sat down for a game together," the first man said. "You are always climbing your apple trees. Why don't you climb over this fence to my side."

"No, I cannot," the second man replied. "I have grown too old for climbing. You have your ax for cutting firewood. Why don't you get your ax and chop a bit of this fence down?"

"I cannot," he said. "This fence took so long to build, and now I have no more energy for tearing it down."

As the friends looked at each other, they suddenly felt very old indeed. Without another word, they turned and went into their homes. As the first man sat before his warm fireplace, he thought about how nice it would be to sip a cup of sweet cider with his friend beside him.

The second man went into his house and poured himself a mug of cider. He sat before his empty hearth to drink it and found that his house was lonely and cold.

IN the story of the two old men, the fence the men built created deep barriers of mistrust and anger. Before the two friends had the fence, they worked and played games as friends. But as time went by, they became more involved with the fence that divided them than with the garden that brought them together. Finally their garden died because they could only see their separation. They forgot about how they used to love and respect each other and instead became angry and suspicious of each other.

RESPECTING DIFFERENCE

Think about these proverbs:

"One man's trash is another
   man's treasure."
"Different strokes for different
   folks."
"Live and let live."
"Half the world does not know
   how the other half lives."

Eventually, they could no longer communicate and chose to live apart rather than do the hard work of pulling down the fence and rebuilding their friendship.

In this story, fences are bad. They are metaphors for all that separates us from our fellow human beings. However, do you think this is the meaning that this proverb originally was intended to convey?

In fact, New England farmers created this proverb to express the wisdom of respecting the boundary lines between neighbors. In today's world, few of us may have farmland and woods that border another's property—but we can all benefit from setting healthy limits around our lives. No one should be allowed to trespass on our personal rights—anymore than we should invade another's privacy.

There is a big difference between a fence and a high wall. But since most of us no longer live in rural farming communities, we may no longer recognize this difference. In cases like these, where our world has changed since the time when the proverb was created, we may not always immediately understand the wisdom an old proverb offers.

THE IGNORANCE OF ONE BECOMES THE IGNORANCE OF MANY

In other cases, however, our world has changed for the better. What past generations perceived as wisdom, we now recognize as falsehood. Although many proverbs encourage thoughtfulness and understanding, a few proverbs are based on fear and ignorance.

Like the two men in the story, people often build harmful

Do you think the following proverbs are positive or negative? How has our world changed since these "words of wisdom" were created?

"A woman's place is in the home."
"Beggars can't be choosers."
"Children should be seen and not heard."

fences between each other. These fences are not necessarily physical. Proverbs based on fear and ignorance build fences between people by encouraging **stereotypes** and **prejudice**. They do this by pointing out people's differences in hurtful and insulting ways. There are even many proverbs that are based on hate. Hate drives barriers between people that are stronger than any physical fence could ever be.

One of the most extreme, hateful, and **racist** proverbs in American tradition is, "The only good Indian is a dead Indian." Fortunately, this saying is rarely heard in America today. But even one person repeating a hateful and ignorant statement like this is too many.

We need to understand the negative elements of our history, so that we can work to overcome them. Many people believe this negative saying originated in 1869, when General Philip Sheridan of the United States Union Army and a hero of the Civil War said these awful words to Chief Tosawi of the Comanche. Others believe the saying began in 1868 when James Michael Cavanagh from Montana said this racist phrase to the United States House of Representatives.

In some ways, it does not matter when this terrible saying began. Far more important is the way the saying quickly spread among white people in North America. The "proverb" became a slogan supporting the killing of millions of Native Americans, while it encouraged moving those who were left onto reservations where many Native Americans still live in poverty today.

This so-called proverb became an even more common part of American language as it was adapted and used in numerous other racist contexts over the years. The proverb was applied to

Sometimes proverbs can help cut through prejudice by helping other members of society better understand the value and insight of a particular ethnic group. Here are some proverbs that reveal the wisdom and culture of African Americans.

Brick top of brick makes house.
The deeper you dig, the richer the soil.
Every tub must sit on its own bottom.
Fingers are not equal.
It takes two birds to make a nest.
You run with dogs, you catch fleas.
The littlest snowflakes make the deepest snow.
The bird can't fly with one wing.
Feed the devil with a *long* spoon.
If you don't want to trade with the devil, keep out of his shop.
If you play with dogs, you get bitten.
A snake may change his skin, but he's still a snake.
The gourd will follow the vine.

African Americans, to Germans in World War II, and to the Vietnamese in the Vietnam War, just to name a few.

Proverbs based on stereotypes and ignorance are very dangerous, not only because of their cruelty, but also because they encourage people to form negative ideas about people who are different from themselves. Racist proverbs erase the humanity of the targeted group by stripping the people of their dignity and individuality. They also smear the humanity of the speaker by revealing his ignorance, prejudice, and cruelty.

The next time you hear a proverb, ask yourself, "What does this proverb mean?" "What will happen if I repeat this proverb?" "Whose feelings might it hurt?" "Would I be happy if someone said this about me?" Sometimes a "good" proverb can be used to support a stereotype or to make a hurtful judgment on an individual.

Remember, just because other people say it, doesn't mean it is necessarily good or true. After all, as the old proverbial question goes, "If everyone else jumped off a bridge, would you?"

The Sphinx in the story of Oedipus Rex will be forever associated with life's most mysterious riddles.

SIX

Riddles and Wisdom
A Somber Riddle in One of the
Oldest of Folktales

Can you solve this riddle: How much dirt is in a hole that is 4 feet deep and 2 feet wide?
Answer: None. (There is no dirt in a hole.)

OEDIPUS SUFFERED from a clouded fate from the moment he was born. His father was the King of Thebes and his mother was the Queen, so his life should have been filled with fun and luxury, but Oedipus' future brewed like a dark storm.

When Oedipus was still a baby, a **soothsayer** told the king that Oedipus would grow up to kill him and marry the Queen, Oedipus' own mother. The King believed what the soothsayer told him and decided that Oedipus must be killed instead. Of course, the King could not kill his own son, so he ordered a servant to take the harmless looking baby boy away and kill him.

Now, the servant knew that he should follow orders—but he looked at the baby, smiling and gurgling in his arms, and he could not bring himself to kill the helpless little creature. Instead, he left Oedipus out in the wilderness with only the Winds of Fate to guide him.

Oedipus was found and brought to a city far from Thebes, where he was adopted and lived a full and happy life. Then one day, tragedy struck. Again, a soothsayer appeared with a frightening tale. The soothsayer told Oedipus that he was destined to kill his father and marry his mother. Oedipus was horrified. He loved his parents very much and would never dream of doing anything to harm them. How could this possibly be true? Fearing for his parents' lives and happiness, he decided he would do anything to save them from his terrible fate, so he packed all of his belongings and left them forever.

As fate would have it, Oedipus found himself traveling on the road to Thebes. On that day, the King also happened to be

traveling along the same road, and when their wagons met, a great fight ensued. Each man refused to move for the other man. They insulted each other and came to blows. In the blink of an eye, the King, Oedipus' own father, was dead. But Oedipus did not know that the man he killed was actually his father and continued confidently on his way.

The city of Thebes, however, toward which Oedipus was headed, was in great distress. A horrible, frightening creature, the **Sphinx**, was blocking entrance to the city. Anyone who wished to enter needed to answer the riddle of the Sphinx. If he could not, the Sphinx would kill him. But the Sphinx was a wise and supernatural creature, and no one knew the answer to the Sphinx's riddle. No one could pass, but many were killed.

Oedipus had always been known for his intelligence. He was confident that he could answer the Sphinx's riddle, so he took the challenge. The Sphinx looked upon Oedipus and asked the

The word "riddle" comes from an Old English word that had to do with conjecturing, forming an opinion, interpreting. Interestingly, it comes from a similar word root as the word "read." How do you think reading and riddling might be related?

great riddle, "What animal walks on four feet in the morning, two feet at noon, and three feet in the evening?"

For a moment it seemed that Oedipus might not know the answer. His brow furrowed in thought. Then he spoke, "It is man. Man crawls on hands and knees when young, walks on two legs when an adult, and needs a cane when he is old."

The Sphinx had been outwitted and died in disbelief and shame. The road to Thebes was safe again, and Oedipus the great, wise man married the Queen (his true mother) and became king himself, thus unwittingly fulfilling the destiny the Fates had proclaimed.

The story of Oedipus Rex (also called Oedipus the King) is one of the Greek tragic myths. Written into a play by Sophocles, this story has been told so many times down through history that it has become a part of our folk myths, one of the enduring examples of stories that teach important lessons for people's lives. However, in addition to the other lessons this story teaches, it also shows an example of the role riddles can play in literature and life.

As in this story, knowledge is often respected more and considered to be more powerful than physical strength. But knowledge also provides its own challenges. Knowledgeable people often demand that others think critically about their beliefs and practices. But sometimes people do not wish to question themselves or change their ways (especially if it would mean admitting that they were wrong).

Socrates, an ancient Greek philosopher born around 470 BC, did not simply ask riddles

FIVE ANCIENT RIDDLES

"At night they come without being fetched,
And by day they are lost without being stolen."
Hint: They belong to the night.

"I never was, am always to be,
No one ever saw me, nor ever will
And yet I am the confidence of all
To live and breathe on this terrestrial ball."
Hint: It never comes

"Runs over fields and woods all day
Under the bed at night sits not alone,
With long tongue hanging out,
A-waiting for a bone."
Hint: It's something very close to you.

"The beginning of eternity
The end of time and space
The beginning of every end,
And the end of every place."
Hint: It's in front of you right now.

"There was a green house.
Inside the green house there was a white house
Inside the white house there was a red house.
Inside the red house there were lots of babies."
Hint: A fruit

(*Answers:* the stars; tomorrow; a shoe; the letter "e"; a watermelon)

for fun. His riddles were deep, and often unanswerable, questions about existence and the meaning of life. He was always challenging people to think, and it got him into trouble. Finally, he was arrested and given a choice: he could be executed, or choose to commit suicide. Socrates chose suicide and drank a cup of hemlock juice (a powerful poison) while his followers sat mournfully around him.

Because Socrates' strength was in his mind, not his body, his strength did not die with him. Instead, his followers carried on

SOME JEWISH RIDDLES

It's not a shirt—
Yet it's sewed;
It's not a tree—
Yet it's full of leaves;
It's not a person—
Yet it talks sensibly.
What is it?

Answer: A book.

A person dreamed he was on a ship at sea with his father and his mother and that the ship had begun to sink. It was, however, impossible to save both of his parents; he could save either his father or his mother—but not both. What should he do?

Answer: He should wake up.

SOME JEWISH CONUNDRUMS

What is it that everyone wants, but when they get it
   they don't like it?
Answer: Old age.

Who can speak in all languages?
Answer: Echo.

What causes us neither pain nor sorrow yet makes us
   weep?
Answer: Onions.

What does a pious Jew do before he drinks tea?
Answer: He opens his mouth.

What kind of water can you carry in a sieve?
Answer: Frozen water.

What live creatures were not on Noah's Ark?
Answer: Fish.

his teachings. We still study Socrates in school today, and one of
his teachings, "An unexamined life is not worth living" has become a widely used proverb.

The Sphinx's riddle in the story of Oedipus Rex is a challenge
to all people who believe they are wise. This riddle is not simply
for fun. The Sphinx's life, and the life of the challenger, is de-
pendent upon the answer to the riddle. The Sphinx cannot be
killed or moved by any other means than solving her riddle. In

this story, knowledge is the greatest form of power. Oedipus' success with this riddle proves that he is a man of the greatest wisdom, so great that he is made king. However, in this story we also see that even the wisest man is not free from fate and folly, for even with all his wisdom, Oedipus is unable to escape what was predicted at his birth. In solving the riddle, Oedipus shows that he is very strong in intelligence, but his ignorance about who his true parents are and what he has done makes him very weak in other ways.

The story of Oedipus Rex also shows us that riddles come in many different forms. Oedipus can solve the riddle the Sphinx poses, but he is unaware of the larger riddle of his life. Riddles can come in almost any form, all the way from the simplest rhymes we ask each other in childhood, to the most complex questions that philosophers ponder. Furthermore, not every riddle has a prescribed answer. The answer to "Why did the chicken cross the road?" is almost ridiculous in its simplicity: "To get to the other side." But the answer to the greatest riddle of all, "What is the meaning of life?" is something every human has pondered and probably no human will ever completely solve.

Farmer John raises pigs!

SEVEN

A Humorous and Questioning Mind

A Variety of Conundrums, Puzzles, and Word Games

"What happens to a white rock when you throw it into the Red Sea?"

JANICE'S FAVORITE thing in all the world was riddles. She could sit all day, pondering a riddle, feeling her brain twisting and turning, pretzel-like with the challenge, searching for the answer.

Every day, Janice couldn't wait until her mom came home from work with the newspaper in her hand. Janice would rush for the door and tear the paper from her mother's grip. She ripped through its inky pages to find the day's crossword puzzle. Janice thought crossword puzzles were one of the best types of riddles.

Janice would take the riddles she found and challenge her friends with them. "Hey Todd," she would ask, "What has four legs and goes oom, oom?"

"I don't know," said Todd.

"A cow going backwards!" Janet gleefully replied. "Hey Peggy! What's older than the earth and sky, will always be around, and won't ever die?"

"I don't know," said Peggy.

"Time! The answer is time!"

Janice even searched for riddles on television. Her favorite television show was *Jeopardy*. She loved trying to shout out the answers before the players did. She wasn't very good at it yet, but she knew that in a few years, she'd have them all beat!

Janice liked almost anything that challenged her mind. The one thing, however, that Janice did not like was going to school. She knew school was also supposed to challenge her mind, but she thought school was terribly boring. The lessons, chapters, and exams never seemed as interesting as her riddles.

But then one day in math class, Janet made an amazing discovery. The class was doing word problems. "School starts at 8:00 A.M. It takes Greg ten minutes to shower, and four minutes to brush his teeth. It takes him another 15 minutes to get dressed, eat breakfast, and gather his schoolbooks. Then Greg has a 17-minute ride to school. What time does Greg need to wake up by in order to be at school at eight?"

At first Janice stared at the problem with no idea what to do. But then a thought struck her. *Wait a minute!* Janice thought, *This question is a little like a riddle. I'm great at riddles! This should be no problem!* Janice thought about the problem. *First you need to know how much time Greg takes to get from his bed to school;* so she added all the numbers up. *Forty-six. Greg takes 46 minutes to get from his bed to school. If there are 60 minutes in an hour, then Greg would have to get up at 7:14 to be at school at 8:00.* Janice was so proud of herself that she couldn't wait to get to the next problem.

Not every question is a riddle, of course. But riddles appeal to human curiosity. They carry the implication that problem-solving can be fun. Science class, Janice noticed, asked her to use her brain in a similar way. In history, she also realized she enjoyed her lessons more when she used both her curiosity and her problem-solving skills.

"In fourteen-hundred-and-ninety-two, who sailed the ocean blue? Columbus!"

From now on, Janice thought, she was going to make school a lot more fun.

A HISTORICAL RIDDLE

Many myths about me abound,
Like I cut a cherry tree right down,
But what is completely true is that
I was America's first president.

Who am I?

Answer: George Washington

Sometimes learning doesn't seem like fun, but through riddles, puzzles, and word games, people have traditionally challenged their minds without even realizing the intellectual benefits to their games. In fact, a lot of the joy in education

depends on what perspective a person has toward education. If we look at learning as a chore that is required of us, then it will probably feel like a chore. If we look at learning, however, as an opportunity and a challenge, then it may feel different. Riddles are an important part of our folklore; they carry within them a tradition of curiosity and play—and when we apply this perspective to academic learning, it can make school a whole lot more fun!

TRICKY PUZZLES

Some riddles try to trick the listener by using complicated, wordy ways of asking a question. For example:

> *"Farmer John had 12 pigs. He gave four to his neighbor Jill and three to his friend Farmer Brown. Jill only needed one, so she gave one to Farmer Brown and gave the rest back to Farmer John. Then Farmer John took three more to the butcher in town. How many cows does Farmer John have left?"*

Using the oral tradition to quickly deliver this type of riddle prevents the recipient from being able to read the riddle and care-

The secret to escaping from a cement room with no doors or windows!

fully scrutinize what has actually been said. Instead, he must rely on good listening and reasoning skills. Because the recipient is busy trying to keep track of a complicated scenario of events and is trying to understand and remember all of the math involved in counting the pigs, the person often misses the very simple solution to the riddle.

(*Answer:* No cows. Farmer John raises pigs.)

Learning does not, of course, only happen in classrooms when we are young. Opportunities for learning abound all throughout our lives, in and out of the classroom. Some of a per-

son's most important lessons may happen in a library, observing people on the street, watching the news, looking at a piece of art, or talking to people. There are always new things to learn and educational opportunities around all the time.

Lots of adults find that with things like work, bills, and family, their lives are too hectic for the type of learning that comes from reading long books or taking a class at a local university. Crossword puzzles in the local newspaper, television shows like *Jeopardy,* and games like Trivial Pursuit are great ways for people to keep their brains sharp and learn while still having fun.

Can you write your own conundrums using words that sound alike? Try some of these words:

deer, dear

week, weak

meet, meat

rain, reign

prey, pray

feet, feat

grate, great

son, sun

wait, weight

A RIDDLE A DAY KEEPS BRAINROT AWAY!

Some riddles have their answer hidden in the clue:

1. A farmer had five cows. All but two died. How many cows were left?
2. At a railroad crossing, look for cars;
   Can you spell all that without any R's?
4. If a rooster laid square eggs, what kind of chicks would hatch?

A CONFUSING PROBLEM

Three merchants and three robbers had to cross a lake. However, only one rowboat was available, and it was only big enough to care two people at a time. How could they all manage to get across, since each of the merchants was afraid of being left alone with two robbers?

Answer: First of all two robbers crossed. One robber then brought the boat back and rowed across the third robber. Then the robber returned once more and remained on shore while two merchants got in the boat and rowed across. A merchant with one robber returned with the boat, and the robber got out so that the two merchants could row across. A robber on the other side returned to fetch the robber who had got out.

Answers:
1. 2 cows (all *but* 2 died)
2. a-l-l-t-h-a-t (the question asks if you can spell the words "all that"
3. None (roosters don't lay eggs)

Now that you've had some practice, can you solve these?

1. What kind of bushes do animals hide under when it rains?
2. What happens to a white rock when your throw it into the Red Sea?
3. Though you push it
   In the same place
   It flies with you
   At a great pace.
4. What has eyes but never cries?

Answers:
1. Wet bushes
2. It sinks
3. A bicycle
4. A potato

"What kind of bushes do animals hide under when it rains?"

CONFUSING CONUNDRUMS

1. Why is 6 afraid of 7?
2. You are in a cement room with no windows and no doors. The only things you have are a mirror and a piece of wood. How can you escape from this room?

Answers:
1. Because 7 8 9 (because 7 *ate* 9)
2. First look in the mirror to see what you saw. Now take the saw and cut the piece of wood in half because two halves make a whole. Take your two halves and escape through the hole.

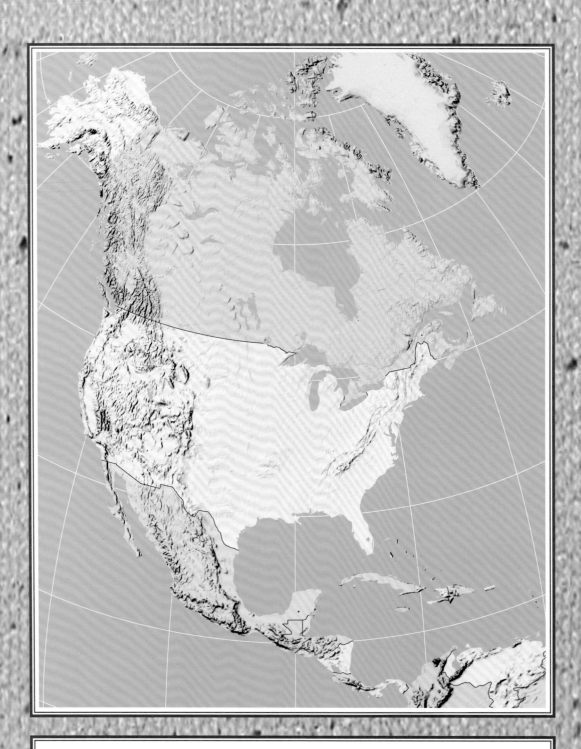

From Canada in the north down through Mexico in the south, the folk riddles and proverbs of North America have unique flavors all their own.

EIGHT

From Canada
to Mexico
Regional and Ethnic Proverbs
and Riddles

"Great trees keep little ones down," is an example of an American proverb.

IN 1993, Canada, the United States, and Mexico signed NAFTA, the North American Free Trade Agreement. The goal of NAFTA was to increase trade within North America that could be economically beneficial to all three countries involved.

NAFTA is only one example of the many trends, social, political, and economic, that are part of what we call "globalization." Globalization is a term used to refer to the current situation in the world in which countries are joining together in ever increasing numbers through political, military, and economic networks and alliances. Though individual countries' physical borders still exist, globalization increases a country's contact with and reliance upon other nations of the world.

NAFTA is one example of an economic network being created between countries, but many other things are shared between countries as well. The sharing and spread of information and ideas is another example of the impact of globalization. Things like televisions, telephones, the Internet, satellites, and fax machines all allow information to pass almost instantly from one part of the world to another.

The sharing of ideas from around the world has led to cultural mixing of all kinds. Today, American children can watch Japanese animation on their Saturday morning cartoons. An artist in Mexico can display his work via the Internet to a potential buyer in Europe. And during the Olympics, a person in South Africa can watch one of Canada's favorite sports, curling.

With such widespread sharing of ideas and cultures, it can sometimes be difficult to discover where a specific idea or tradition

"A short horse is soon curried" is a proverb from New England.

originated, especially if an idea or tradition has been shared by many different groups for a long time. In North America, ideas like proverbs and riddles have been shared throughout Mexico, the United States, and Canada for much longer than economic agreements like NAFTA have existed.

The proverbs and riddles that are commonly used in North America are not strictly Canadian, Mexican, or American at all. North America has extremely diverse populations made up of people of many different cultures, backgrounds, religions, and beliefs. Throughout our

JEWISH PROVERBS

God governs the whole world. (In other words: All's right with the world).
Man thinks, and God laughs. (In other words: Man proposes and God disposes).

God sends the remedy before the disease. (In other words: God never sends a problem to which he hasn't provided a solution.)

history, immigrants from all over the world have been settling in North America. These people, whose traditions are often older than the countries in which they now live, bring their proverbs, riddles, and other aspects of their culture here with them. Many proverbs that are now commonly used across North America have

"Low man on the totem pole," is a proverb often used in the work world—but it has its roots in Canadian folk tradition.

their roots in much smaller groups and regions.

However, like all forms of folklore, proverbs and riddles can give you a feel for a particular region or culture. Here are some examples.

AMERICAN PROVERBS

"Feel for others, in your pocket."

"You cannot unscramble eggs."

CANADIAN PROVERBS

"The devil places a pillow for drunken men to fall upon."

"Save your breath to cool your porridge."

"She was pure as snow, but she drifted."

An American proverb: "The bad gardener quarrels with his rake."

PROVERBS FROM MASSACHUSETTS

Don't stay till the last dog's hung.

Dunghills rise and castles fall.

Proverbs endure for hundreds, even thousands of years. According to an African proverb from the Ashanti people, "Ancient things remain in the ear."

"You have to kiss a lot of toads before you find a handsome prince" is a modern folk proverb from the United States.

Newfoundland Proverbs

"He'll wish his bread dough."

"A new broom sweeps clean, but it takes an old one for the corners."

"A hug without a kiss is like an egg without salt."

NATIVE AMERICAN PROVERBS

Cheyenne
"Do not judge a man until you have walked two moons in his moccasins." (This saying was adapted and changed in America to *"Do not judge a man until you have walked a mile in his shoes."*)

Crow
"The more you give, the more good things come to you." (This saying was adapted and changed to *"The more you give, the more you get."*)

Ute

"Don't walk behind me;
I may not lead.
Don't walk in front of me;
I may not follow.
Walk beside me that we may be
as one."

Hopi

"The rain falls on the just and
the unjust." (A very similar
proverb is found in the
Judeo-Christian Scriptures.)

PROVERBS FROM NEW MEXICO

(translated from Spanish)

The three evils of this world, that a man can ever suffer,
are to live in another's house, to beg, and to be a pauper.

To see you in another's arms gives me the fever and sweats;
but a saying goes that "God delays but never forgets."

Let no one say in this world, "Of this water I won't drink,"
no matter how muddy it looks, it may quench your thirst.

Dakota

"We will be known forever by the tracks we leave behind."

Omaha

"It is easy to be brave from a distance."

Iowa

"A brave man dies but once, a coward many times."

"What gets wetter the more it dries?
Answer: A tea towel

Proverbs arise from a society's common beliefs, experiences, and values. The sayings that are used in any given place at any given time will usually reflect the current circumstances and conditions in which those people are living. If a society is suffering economic hardship, people may use proverbs about thrift and responsibility like "God helps those who help themselves." If a country is fighting a war, the proverbs people choose to use may focus on themes like loyalty, honor, strength, and national unity, like "United we stand, divided we fall."

Blackfoot

"Those who lie down with dogs, get up with fleas."

Sioux

"The frog does not drink up the pond in which he lives."

Tuscarora

"They are not dead who live in the hearts they leave behind."

Mexican Proverbs

"The sin carries its own penance."

"Let water run that you do not intend to drink."

"A lamp in the street, obscurity at home."

"When you see that someone is cutting your neighbor's beard, start wetting yours."

REGIONAL RIDDLES

It can be difficult to find riddles that have the same history and cultural ties that proverbs have. Part of this is because proverbs are pieces of wisdom that are carried on for generations. Riddles, on the other hand, are used as ways of testing a person's knowledge and are often thought of on the spot. Here are some riddles from children in Canada.

"How do you make anti-freeze?"
Answer: *You put ice in her bed.*

"What do you get when you cross a bear and a skunk?"
Answer: *Winnie the Pee-u!*

Do you think there is anything specifically Canadian about these riddles? What about the riddles that you know? Do they have characteristics from your culture or the region that you live in?

BOTH proverbs and riddles embody a culture's perception of general truths and awareness. Some scholars say that the use of proverbs and riddles is a marker for societies; these forms of folklore indicate the movement of more primitive thinking toward deductive and inductive reasoning. In more primitive societies, proverbs often serve as ethical and legal guides—and even in highly industrialized North America, proverbs have power to shape and maintain group attitudes. Riddles may puzzle us and make us laugh—but both riddles and proverbs make us think.

Further Reading

Bartlett, John. *Bartlett's Familiar Quotations: A Collection of Passages, Phrases, and Proverbs Traced to Their Sources in Ancient and Modern Literature.* New York: Little, Brown, 1992.

Bierhorst, John, editor. *Lightning Inside You: And Other Native American Riddles.* New York: William Morrow, 1992.

Collis, Harry. *101 American English Riddles: Understanding Language and Culture through Humor.* New York: Contemporary Books, 1996.

Cousineau, Phil and Wes Scoop Nisker. *A World Treasury of Riddles.* Berkeley, Calif.: Conari, 2001.

Davis, Mary J. and Barbara Rogers. *My Wisdom Journal: A Discovery of Proverbs for Kids.* San Diego: Legacy, 2000.

Greer, Colin and Herbert Kohl. *A Call to Character: A Family Treasury of Stories, Poems, Plays, Proverbs, and Fables to Guide the Development of Values for You and Your Children.* New York: HarperPerennial, 1997.

Mieder, Wolfgang. *Children and Proverbs Speak the Truth: Teaching Proverbial Wisdom to Fourth Graders.* Burlington: University of Vermont, 2000.

Stewart, Julia. *African Proverbs and Wisdom: A Collection for Every Day of the Year, from More than Forty African Nations.* New York: Kensington, 2002.

Swann, Brian. *Touching the Distance: Native American Riddle-poems.* San Diego: Browndeer Press, 1998.

For More Information

Proverbs

www.oneproverb.com

www.oneliners-and-proverbs.com

www.afriprov.org

www.aitech.ac.jp

www.proverbs.com/

Riddles

www.justriddlesandmore.com

www.fun4children.com

www.niehs.nih.gov/kids/braint/htm

www.riddlenut.com

www.riddles.com

Glossary

Almanac   An annual publication containing miscellaneous information, including statistics and weather information for a given year.

Conundrum   A riddle, often one that has a pun (using words with the same sounds but different meanings to suggest additional meaning) in the answer.

Literal   Having to do with the exact and realistic meaning.

Metaphorical   A way of describing something using another thing that makes sense imaginatively, but not literally. For example, stabbing cold: the word "stabbing" metaphorically describes the feeling of the cold, but cold cannot literally stab.

Oral literature   Stories, tales, poems, records, etc. that are spoken but not written down.

Prejudice   A preconceived opinion; judgments made based on opinions rather than fact or experience.

Racism   A belief that a particular race is better or worse than other races, often leading to prejudice.

Slogan   A brief, attention-getting phrase.

Soothsayer   Fortuneteller.

Sphinx   A winged mythological monster with a human head and a lion's body.

Stereotypes   Preconceived, oversimplified, and standardized impressions applied to a group of people, often ignoring the differences and variability within that group.

Index

Biographies

Autumn Libal is a graduate of Smith College in Northampton, Massachusetts.

Dr. Alan Jabbour is a folklorist who served as the founding director of the American Folklife Center at the Library of Congress from 1976 to 1999. Previously, he began the grant-giving program in folk arts at the National Endowment for the Arts (1974–76). A native of Jacksonville, Florida, he was trained at the University of Miami (B.A.) and Duke University (M.A., Ph.D.). A violinist from childhood on, he documented old-time fiddling in the Upper South in the 1960s and 1970s. A specialist in instrumental folk music, he is known as a fiddler himself, an art he acquired directly from elderly fiddlers in North Carolina, Virginia, and West Virginia. He has taught folklore and folk music at UCLA and the University of Maryland and has published widely in the field.